Avatar

Name:

Address:

Mobile:

Email:

Facebook:

Case Study

Company:

Profile:

Top-Down Analysis

Macro Economy

Industry

Company

SWOT Analysis

Strengths	Weakness
Opportunity	**Threats**

Business Model Canvas

Key Partners

Key Activities

Key Resources

Value Propositions

Customer Relationships

Channels

Customer Segments

Cost Structure

Revenue Streams

Five Forces Analysis

Industry Rivalry and Competitiveness

Threat of New Entrants

Bargaining power of Suppliers

Bargaining power of Customers

Threat of Substitute Product

Revenue and Profit Highlight

Revenue

Cost

Profit

Balance Sheet Highlight

Asset

Liability

Equity

Cash Flow Highlight

Operation

Investing

Financing

Financial Ratio Highlight

Risk:

Cash Cycle:

Return:

Other:

Key Decision

| Invest | Not Invest |

Note

Note

Note

Note

Case Study

Company:

Profile:

Top-Down Analysis

Macro Economy

Industry

Company

SWOT Analysis

Strengths	Weakness
Opportunity	Threats

Business Model Canvas

Key Partners	Cost Structure

Key Activities	Key Resources

Value Propositions

	Revenue Streams

Customer Relationships	Channels

Customer Segments

Five Forces Analysis

Industry Rivalry and Competitiveness

Threat of New Entrants

Bargaining power of Suppliers

Bargaining power of Customers

Threat of Substitute Product

Revenue and Profit Highlight

Revenue

Cost

Profit

Balance Sheet Highlight

Asset

Liability

Equity

Cash Flow Highlight

Operation

Investing

Financing

Financial Ratio Highlight

Risk:

Cash Cycle:

Return:

Other:

Key Decision

| Invest | Not Invest |

Note

Note

Note

Note

Case Study

Company:

Profile:

Top-Down Analysis

Macro Economy

Industry

Company

SWOT Analysis

Strengths	Weakness
Opportunity	Threats

Business Model Canvas

Key Partners	Cost Structure

Key Activities	Key Resources

Value Propositions

Customer Relationships	Channels

Revenue Streams

Customer Segments

Five Forces Analysis

Industry Rivalry and Competitiveness

Threat of New Entrants

Bargaining power of Suppliers

Bargaining power of Customers

Threat of Substitute Product

Revenue and Profit Highlight

Revenue

Cost

Profit

Balance Sheet Highlight

Asset

Liability

Equity

Cash Flow Highlight

Operation

Investing

Financing

Financial Ratio Highlight

Risk:

Cash Cycle:

Return:

Other:

Key Decision

| Invest | Not Invest |

Note

Note

Note

Note

Case Study

Company:

Profile:

Top-Down Analysis

Macro Economy

Industry

Company

SWOT Analysis

Strengths	Weakness
Opportunity	Threats

Business Model Canvas

Key Partners

Key Activities

Key Resources

Value Propositions

Customer Relationships

Channels

Customer Segments

Cost Structure

Revenue Streams

Five Forces Analysis

Industry Rivalry and Competitiveness

Threat of New Entrants

Bargaining power of Suppliers

Bargaining power of Customers

Threat of Substitute Product

Revenue and Profit Highlight

Revenue

Cost

Profit

Balance Sheet Highlight

Asset

Liability

Equity

Cash Flow Highlight

Operation

Investing

Financing

Financial Ratio Highlight

Risk:

Cash Cycle:

Return:

Other:

Key Decision

| Invest | Not Invest |

Note

Note

Note

Note

Case Study

Company:

Profile:

Top-Down Analysis

Macro Economy

Industry

Company

SWOT Analysis

Strengths	Weakness
Opportunity	Threats

Business Model Canvas

Key Partners

Key Activities	Key Resources

Value Propositions

Customer Relationships	Channels

Customer Segments

Cost Structure

Revenue Streams

Five Forces Analysis

Industry Rivalry and Competitiveness

Threat of New Entrants

Bargaining power of Suppliers

Bargaining power of Customers

Threat of Substitute Product

Revenue and Profit Highlight

Revenue

Cost

Profit

Balance Sheet Highlight

Asset

Liability

Equity

Cash Flow Highlight

Operation

Investing

Financing

Financial Ratio Highlight

Risk:

Cash Cycle:

Return:

Other:

Key Decision

Invest	Not Invest

Note

Note

Note

Note

Case Study

Company:

Profile:

Top-Down Analysis

Macro Economy

Industry

Company

SWOT Analysis

Strengths	Weakness
Opportunity	Threats

Business Model Canvas

Key Partners	Cost Structure

Key Activities	Key Resources

Value Propositions

Customer Relationships	Channels

Revenue Streams

Customer Segments

Five Forces Analysis

Industry Rivalry and Competitiveness

Threat of New Entrants

Bargaining power of Suppliers

Bargaining power of Customers

Threat of Substitute Product

Revenue and Profit Highlight

Revenue

Cost

Profit

Balance Sheet Highlight

Asset

Liability

Equity

Cash Flow Highlight

Operation

Investing

Financing

Financial Ratio Highlight

Risk:

Cash Cycle:

Return:

Other:

Key Decision

Invest	Not Invest

Note

Note

Note

Note

Case Study

Company:

Profile:

Top-Down Analysis

Macro Economy

Industry

Company

SWOT Analysis

Strengths	Weakness
Opportunity	Threats

Business Model Canvas

Key Partners

Cost Structure

Key Activities

Key Resources

Value Propositions

Revenue Streams

Customer Relationships

Channels

Customer Segments

Five Forces Analysis

Industry Rivalry and Competitiveness

Threat of New Entrants

Bargaining power of Suppliers

Bargaining power of Customers

Threat of Substitute Product

Revenue and Profit Highlight

Revenue

Cost

Profit

Balance Sheet Highlight

Asset

Liability

Equity

Cash Flow Highlight

Operation

Investing

Financing

Financial Ratio Highlight

Risk:

Cash Cycle:

Return:

Other:

Key Decision

| Invest | Not Invest |

Note

Note

Note

Note

Case Study

Company:

Profile:

Top-Down Analysis

Macro Economy

Industry

Company

SWOT Analysis

Strengths	**Weakness**
Opportunity	**Threats**

Business Model Canvas

| Key Partners |
| Key Activities | Key Resources |
| Value Propositions |
| Customer Relationships | Channels |
| Customer Segments |

Cost Structure

Revenue Streams

Five Forces Analysis

Industry Rivalry and Competitiveness

Threat of New Entrants

Bargaining power of Suppliers

Bargaining power of Customers

Threat of Substitute Product

Revenue and Profit Highlight

Revenue

Cost

Profit

Balance Sheet Highlight

Asset

Liability

Equity

Cash Flow Highlight

Operation

Investing

Financing

Financial Ratio Highlight

Risk:

Cash Cycle:

Return:

Other:

Key Decision

| Invest | Not Invest |

Note

Note

Note

Note

Case Study

Company:

Profile:

Top-Down Analysis

Macro Economy

Industry

Company

SWOT Analysis

Strengths	Weakness
Opportunity	Threats

Business Model Canvas

Key Partners		Cost Structure
Key Activities / **Key Resources**		
Value Propositions		
		Revenue Streams
Customer Relationships / **Channels**		
Customer Segments		

Five Forces Analysis

Industry Rivalry and Competitiveness
Threat of New Entrants
Bargaining power of Suppliers
Bargaining power of Customers
Threat of Substitute Product

Revenue and Profit Highlight

Revenue

Cost

Profit

Balance Sheet Highlight

Asset

Liability

Equity

Cash Flow Highlight

Operation

Investing

Financing

Financial Ratio Highlight

Risk:

Cash Cycle:

Return:

Other:

Key Decision

Invest	Not Invest

Note

Note

Note

Note

Case Study

Company:

Profile:

Top-Down Analysis

Macro Economy

Industry

Company

SWOT Analysis

Strengths	Weakness
Opportunity	Threats

Business Model Canvas

Key Partners	Cost Structure

Key Activities	Key Resources

Value Propositions

Customer Relationships	Channels

Revenue Streams

Customer Segments

Five Forces Analysis

Industry Rivalry and Competitiveness

Threat of New Entrants

Bargaining power of Suppliers

Bargaining power of Customers

Threat of Substitute Product

Revenue and Profit Highlight

Revenue

Cost

Profit

Balance Sheet Highlight

Asset

Liability

Equity

Cash Flow Highlight

Operation

Investing

Financing

Financial Ratio Highlight

Risk:

Cash Cycle:

Return:

Other:

Key Decision

Invest	Not Invest

Note

Note

Note

Note

Case Study

Company:

Profile:

Top-Down Analysis

Macro Economy

Industry

Company

SWOT Analysis

Strengths	Weakness
Opportunity	Threats

Business Model Canvas

Key Partners

Cost Structure

Key Activities

Key Resources

Value Propositions

Revenue Streams

Customer Relationships

Channels

Customer Segments

Five Forces Analysis

Industry Rivalry and Competitiveness

Threat of New Entrants

Bargaining power of Suppliers

Bargaining power of Customers

Threat of Substitute Product

Revenue and Profit Highlight

Revenue

Cost

Profit

Balance Sheet Highlight

Asset

Liability

Equity

Cash Flow Highlight

Operation

Investing

Financing

Financial Ratio Highlight

Risk:

Cash Cycle:

Return:

Other:

Key Decision

Invest	Not Invest

Note

Note

Note

Note

Case Study

Company:

Profile:

Top-Down Analysis

Macro Economy

Industry

Company

SWOT Analysis

Strengths	Weakness
Opportunity	Threats

Business Model Canvas

Key Partners

Key Activities

Key Resources

Value Propositions

Customer Relationships

Channels

Customer Segments

Cost Structure

Revenue Streams

Five Forces Analysis

Industry Rivalry and Competitiveness

Threat of New Entrants

Bargaining power of Suppliers

Bargaining power of Customers

Threat of Substitute Product

Revenue and Profit Highlight

Revenue

Cost

Profit

Balance Sheet Highlight

Asset

Liability

Equity

Cash Flow Highlight

Operation

Investing

Financing

Financial Ratio Highlight

Risk:

Cash Cycle:

Return:

Other:

Key Decision

Invest	Not Invest

Note

Note

Note

Note

www.ingramcontent.com/pod-product-compliance
Lightning Source LLC
Chambersburg PA
CBHW071305220526
45468CB00001B/282